Mandala Messages
Do not fear your potential

Donna K. Bearden

2012

Mandala Messages
Copyright © 2012 Donna K. Bearden
All rights reserved.

Requests for permission should be addressed to
donna.bearden14@gmail.com
www.donnabearden.com

ISBN: 978-0-9854250-0-5

With thanks to

Elaine Sullivan,
Cindy Johnson,
and
Leighton Bearden

May I always look for possibilities
where I least expect them.

CONTENTS

The secret of writing resides in
twin gifts: a sense of abundance,
and the trick of beginning.
                    Kim Stafford
        http://www.kim-stafford.com/

Come on In

What began for me as a simple diversion has become a form of meditation. I was drawn to mandalas because of the kaleidoscope effect — that ooh and ah wonder as patterns evolve. Creating photo mandalas became a way for me to suspend the continuous chatter in my head, often analytical, often going in circles.

Without knowing it, I had stumbled onto a form of spiritual practice that crosses cultural lines. From the Buddhist sand mandalas to the Navajo healing mandalas to the prayer labyrinths and rose windows of the great Christian cathedrals, people have been drawn to circles across the ages in deep, meaningful ways.

While we could talk of history, religion, art, and many other things, I would simply like to share some words that spoke to me as I created these photo mandalas.

May the mandalas speak to you as well.

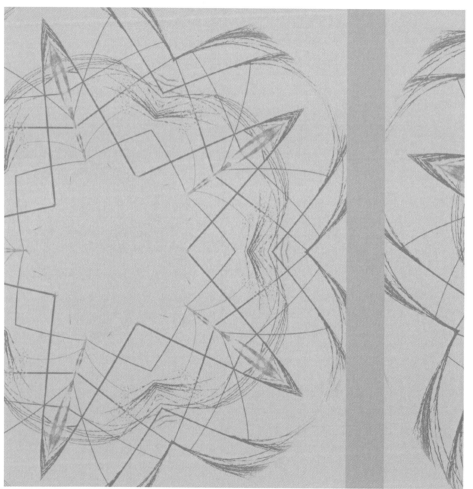

Who am I?

2

If I hide behind the mask
I show to the world
and you hide behind a mask
you have chosen,
Who are we?

I'll put mine down if you will too.

You go first

4

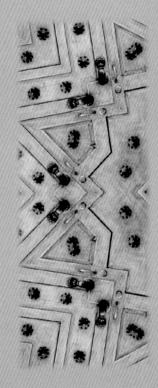

My door isn't always open.
I'm an introvert
and often need solitude.
But knock gently
and if I don't answer today,
please come back.

(Oh, but sometimes
be bold and knock loudly!)

6

I believe there's an artist
in each one of us
Maybe not a capital A Artist
but at least a little a artist who
would love to come out and play

8

Do not fear your potential.
It is a gift to be nurtured,
the best gift you
have been given,
the best gift to share
with the world.

10

Your greatest strength
is your greatest weakness,
she told me.

The trick is to learn
which it is at the time.

What if I *AM* good enough?

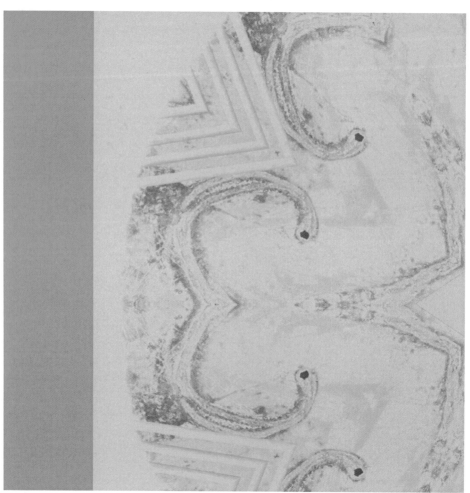

14

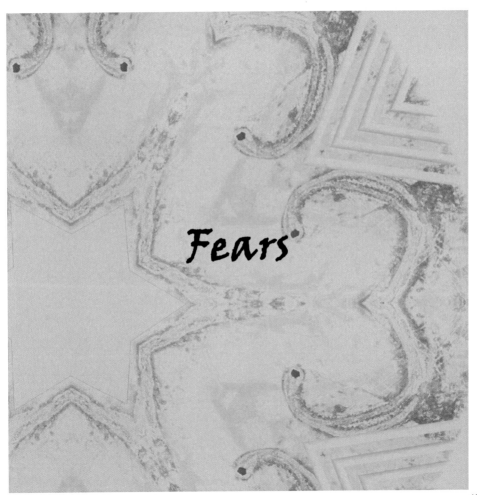

Fears

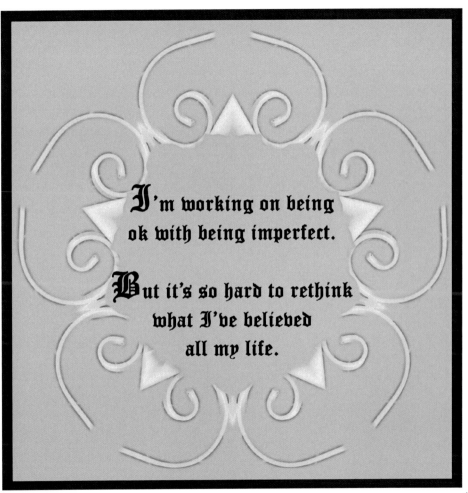

I'm working on being
ok with being imperfect.

But it's so hard to rethink
what I've believed
all my life.

18

If I don't try, I can't fail.
If I don't reach out my hand,
I can't be rejected.
If I don't ..., I can't ....

It's so scary sometimes.

At times I'm a big, fat
scaredy-cat and I want
someone to hold my hand
and help me cross the street.

20

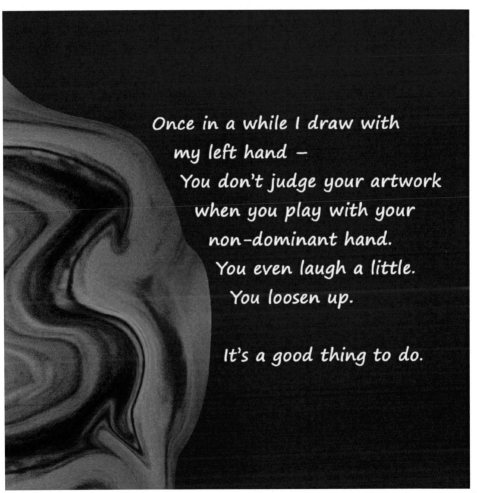

Once in a while I draw with
my left hand —
You don't judge your artwork
when you play with your
non-dominant hand.
You even laugh a little.
You loosen up.

It's a good thing to do.

Listening

24

When someone deeply listens to you
it is like holding out a dented cup
you've had since childhood
and watching it fill up with
cold, fresh water.

John Fox

(When Someone Deeply Listens to You)

26

Your thinking
gets in the way,
she said.

Learn to listen
with the ear of your heart.

Path

30

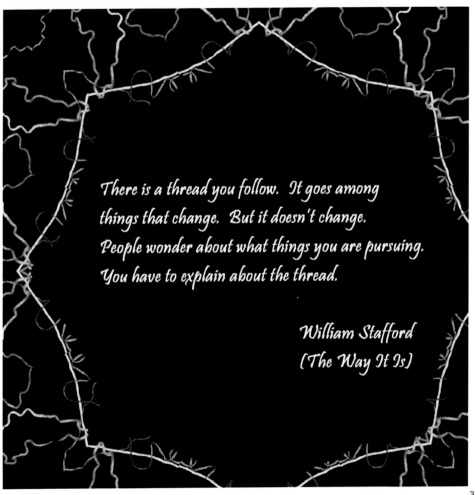

There is a thread you follow. It goes among
things that change. But it doesn't change.
People wonder about what things you are pursuing.
You have to explain about the thread.

William Stafford
(The Way It Is)

32

Just when I am quite sure
of myself, I trip on a root
that sends me sprawling
and nothing looks the
same.

Where was it I
was going?

34

It's easy to get lost
in the branches
and twigs of life,
and forget to see
the patterns
and paths.

36

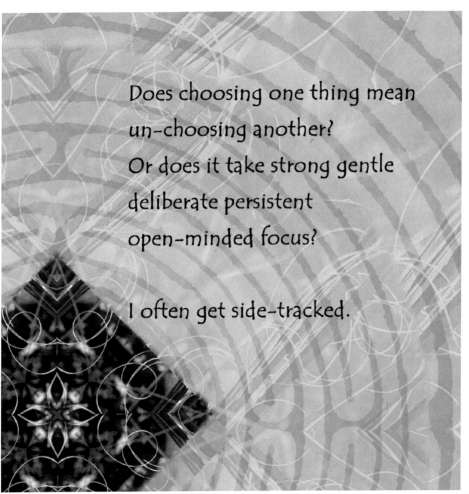

Does choosing one thing mean
un-choosing another?
Or does it take strong gentle
deliberate persistent
open-minded focus?

I often get side-tracked.

Think in terms of practice, she said.
Just like you practice the piano.
Each day you get better.
It's the same with love
and courage
and joy.
Each day you get better.
But you have to practice.
Every day.

40

Was I going out to go in?
Or going in to go out?
Sometimes I get lost in
the busyness and can't
remember which path to
follow.

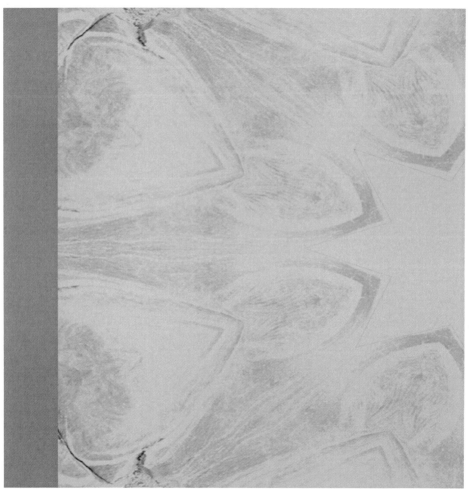

Gratitude

44

Slow down, he said.
Don't miss the sacred moments.
They're all around you,
but so often we hurry past without noticing.
I walked in the forest by the old dead trees.
If not for his words,
I might have missed the dancers.

46

Wake up!
What? I am awake.
Look – a rainbow!
Where? The sky is clear.
There! In the sprinkler!
Don't miss it!

48

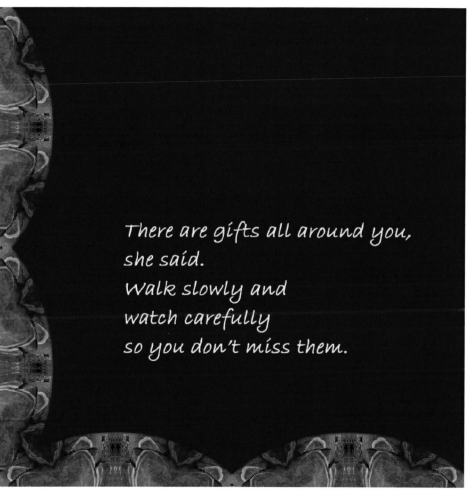

There are gifts all around you,
she said.
Walk slowly and
watch carefully
so you don't miss them.

50

Mystery

Something touches me deep
inside and the tears come all
the way from my toes. That's
what happened when I saw
the rock wall rising from the
desert. I knew I'd been there
before. But I was seeing it
for the first time.

Little spider, do
you choose the
rainbow colors
you spin?
Do you watch
them shimmer
in the morning
dew?
Or is it just all
in a day's work
for you?

I'm looking for just the right words to describe our friendship, she said.
But that's impossible I told her. It can't be reduced to mere words.

58

Forgiveness? she said.
Nothing to it.
Wade through the poison,
wrestle with your ego,
let it go.
Nothing to it.

She's such a story-teller.

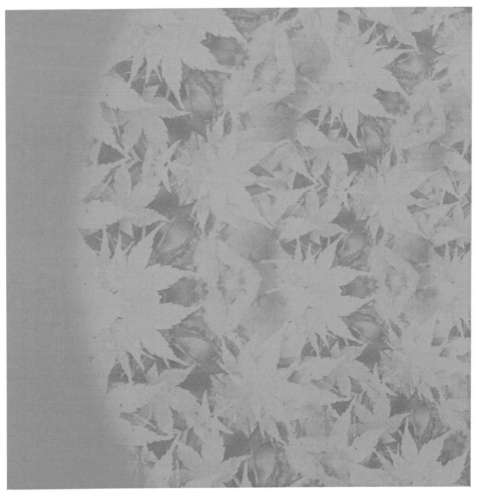

60

Seasons

Can you believe it?
Once again she put on all
her fancy clothes
then shed them in piles
all around.
Such a tease.

Unabashed!
Unashamed!
Extravagant!

Please forgive me
when I think and
act too small.

66

THE TREES STRIP
THEMSELVES
BARE TO BEGIN
ANEW.
WHAT MUST I
LOSE TO MAKE
ROOM FOR
SOMETHING NEW?

68

It's brown and bare
outside and I notice
textures and patterns
that I overlook in lusher
seasons.
So it is with my life.
It is within the valleys
and the shadows that I
notice new perspectives.

In midwinter, when trees are bare and shadows long, sometimes I forget to remember the seeds lying dormant in the cold hard ground.

72

I can't decide, she said,
whether to put on my winter coat
or dress for spring.

Transitions are like that.

Little sprigs and sprouts and touches of green. It's coming! Did you notice?

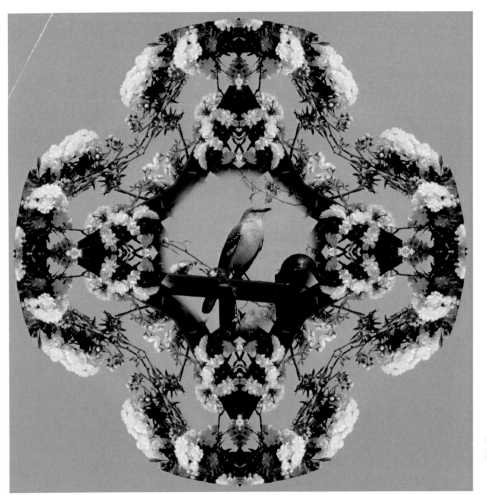

The roses would have been enough.
Then the mockingbird came
to sing his joy to spring.
We shared a sacred moment.

The more I recklessly abandon my fears,
the more I am overwhelmed with gratitude.

Bouquets!
Everywhere I look I see them.
The days are golden!

Donna Bearden's mandala designs are also
available on silk scarves and other items. See:
www.donnabearden.com